Copyright Page

Greatest Dad Ever: Expressions of Gratitude

Written by Kim Ruff Moore

Published by Ruff Moore Media

Book cover illustration by Kim Ruff Moore

Printed in the United States

For more information, visit:

www.kimruffmoore.com

www.ruffmooremedia.com

ISBN 979-8-3302-1318-4

To All The Dads in the world.
Keep being great!

**Other Titles by
Kim Ruff Moore:**
"Suzzie Mocha Series"
"Kirby the Koala Series"
"Sergio the Studio Mouse Series"
"Spence Seven Series"
"Harper Sharper Series"
"Pavo the Parrot"
"Otis the Brave Brown Bear"
"Rosie and the Easter Egg Hunt"
"The Land of Unicorns Series"
"Bria Gets New Braids For
School"
"Elo The Elephant Forgets
Everything"
"Piper The Pretty Pink Dinosaur
Series"
"Kids Prayers Series"
"Mommy, I Can Do It Series"
"Afton Discovers Juneteenth"
"You Are Humongous"

Greatest Dad Ever: Expressions of Gratitude

by Kim Ruff- Moore

In Greatest Dad Ever, Kim Ruff Moore brings together a heartwarming collection of affirmations and stories from children expressing their deep gratitude and love for their fathers. This touching compilation highlights the unique bond between dads and their kids, showcasing the myriad ways fathers contribute to their families. Each page is filled with genuine and heartfelt messages that celebrate the everyday heroism, wisdom, and unconditional love that fathers provide. Perfect for Father's Day or any day, this book is a beautiful tribute to the irreplaceable role that dads play in our lives.

"My dad is the strongest because he can carry me and my sister at the same time."

"I love my dad because he takes me to the zoo and we see all the animals."

ZOO

"Dad always helps me with golf and tells me I'm a great player."

"Dad takes me fishing, and we have so much fun together."

"My dad is the best because he believes in me and makes me feel special."

"I love my dad because he makes the best hamburgers on Saturday evenings."

"Daddy always reads me bedtime stories, and I love the funny voices he makes."

"My dad is my hero because he fixes everything and knows all the answers."

"Dad takes us on vacation and It's my favorite thing to do!" We have so much fun!

"I love playing soccer with my dad. He says I'm the best player."

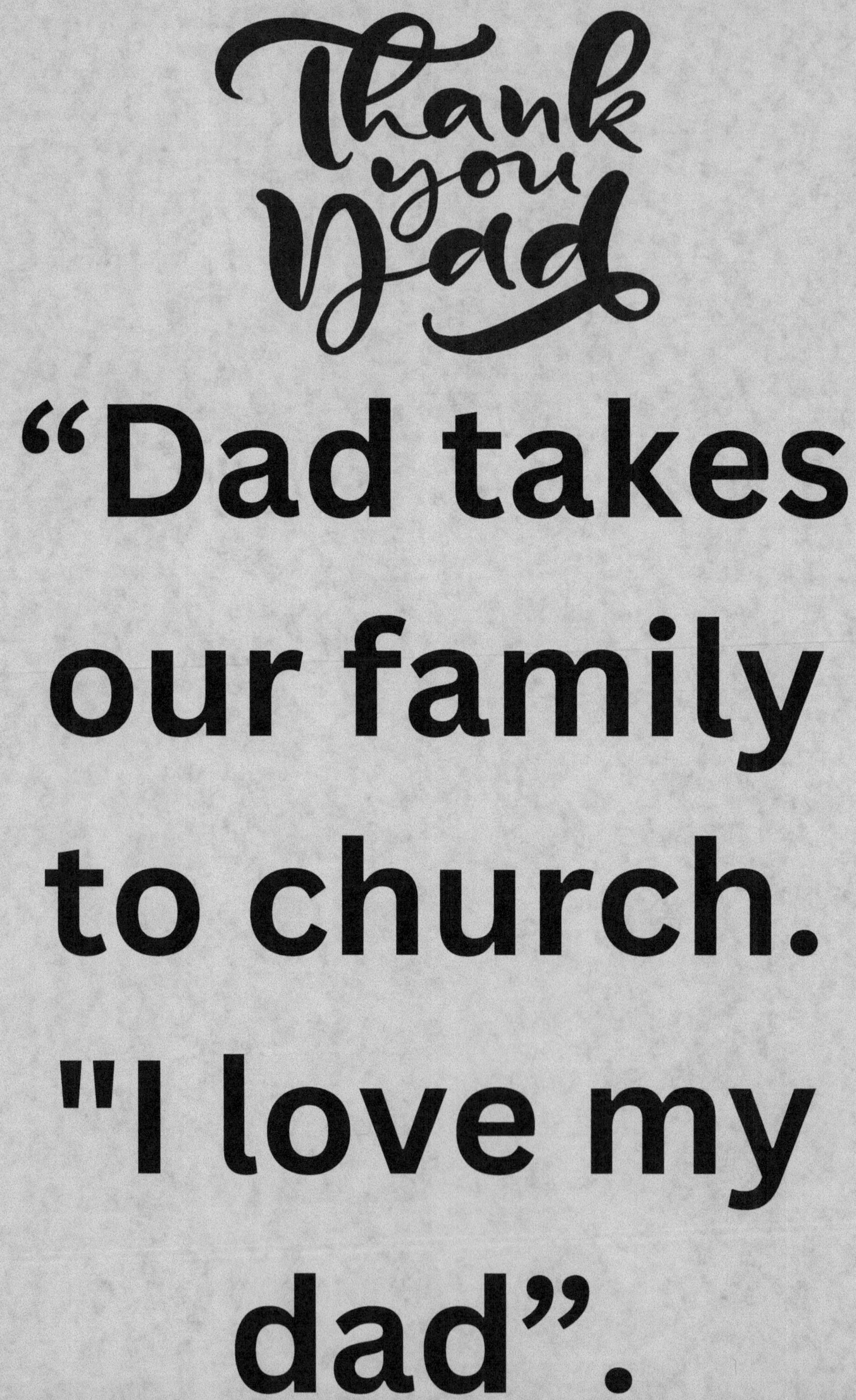

Thank you Dad
"Dad takes our family to church.
"I love my dad".

"My dad is the coolest because he lets me ride on his back."

"Dad always listens to my stories, even when he's busy."

"Thank you to all the wonderful dads who make every day special. Your love, support, and dedication are appreciated more than words can express. "

Epilogue
Greatest Dad Ever
By Kim Ruff Moore

As I sit back and reflect on the heartfelt affirmations and loving tributes within this compilation, I am reminded of the profound impact that our celebrations and holidays have on our lives. This book, "Greatest Dad Ever," was created to honor the incredible contributions of fathers and to celebrate the joy and connection that special days bring to our families.

Life is a series of moments, both big and small, and it's in these moments that we find the true essence of being part of a family. Holidays and celebrations serve as beautiful reminders to pause, appreciate, and cherish the people who mean the most to us. They provide us with the opportunity to express our love, gratitude, and admiration in ways that strengthen our bonds and create lasting memories.

Fathers play a unique and irreplaceable role in the family. They are our protectors, teachers, and heroes. They show us through their actions what it means to be strong, caring, and devoted. Whether it's fixing a broken toy, making us laugh with silly voices, or teaching us how to build and create, dads are there every step of the way, guiding us with their wisdom and love.

In creating this book, I wanted to highlight all that dads do for their families. Their contributions often go unnoticed in the hustle and bustle of daily life, but they are the bedrock upon which many families stand. This compilation of affirmations is a testament to the love and respect that children have for their fathers, showcasing the myriad ways in which dads make a difference.

As you turn the final pages of this book, I hope you are filled with the same sense of warmth and appreciation that I felt while putting it together. Let it serve as a reminder to celebrate the wonderful fathers in our lives, not just on Father's Day, but every day. Let's take the time to acknowledge their efforts, express our gratitude, and make every day the greatest day ever.

Thank you for joining me on this journey of celebration and appreciation. May you find joy in the little moments, and may your life be filled with many more greatest days ever.

With love and gratitude,
Kim Ruff Moore

Kim Ruff Moore is a true Renaissance woman, celebrated as both a gifted author and a Stellar Award-winning singer-songwriter. With over 60 children's books and 12 books for adults to her name, she has established herself as a prolific and versatile writer whose works span across various genres and age groups.

Beyond her literary accomplishments, Kim is also a prominent figure in the music industry. As part of the phenomenal husband and wife duo, The New Consolers, alongside her husband Jeffrey Moore, Kim's soul-stirring performances have captivated audiences worldwide.

Kim's books, imbued with her passion for storytelling and commitment to spreading positivity, have made a significant impact globally. Through her words, she inspires readers of all ages to embrace their creativity, pursue their dreams, and make a difference in the world.